Quirky Verse *from a* Poet Manqué

JJ Secker

First published in May 2018
by Doplin Books, Brighton
www@doplinbooks.com

Production Editor: Xanna Eve Chown
Illustrations: Xanna Eve Chown

ISBN-13:
978-1718666276

ISBN-10:
1718666276

Dedicated to you
[*Add selection of platitude*]
The Magnificent Two
With affection and gratitude

Contents

Amuse-mémoire

A mnemonic verse

I dallied with the Muses, I caressed each lovely Ars,
With Clio I made history, with Urania touched the stars.
I wrung sighs from Melpomene, caused Thalia's laugh to ring,
Made music with Euterpe, had Terpsi' dance and sing.
Calliope was epic, Polyhymnia was sublime,
But it's – oh! – my rare Erato fills my head and bed with rhyme.

Introduction

A verseless voice

Maths

Welcome, both of you, to my life in Verse. Yes, you, who know nothing about me but have bought this slim volume and are reading the introduction, and your fellow traveller whom you probably don't know either. To yourself you are real (if you doubt it reach up and tweak your own nose) but to me you are a combination of mathematics and pop psychology. Allow me to explain.

1.   In a recent study, it was revealed that only 40% of readers looked at the introduction to any book.
2.   Uninformed opinion tells me that, omitting friends who are morally blackmailed into buying it and those who are presented with a copy willynilly, the maximum number liable to buy a book by an unknown poet is ten.
3.   Social observation guarantees that a title containing as pretentious a word as *manqué* cuts this number by at least half.
4.   Half of ten is five: 40% of five is two. Et voilà!
5.   So hello and thanks. This book is dedicated to you (q.v.)

Masefield

Poetry has always fascinated me. At the age of ten, a friend and I wrote a letter to John Masefield who was then Poet Laureate. His 'Cargoes' was, and still is, one of my favourite pieces of poesy: How three identical verses through a careful selection of words can change rhythm to mirror the movement of each ship is pure poetic magic.

Even greater magic was the fact that he replied to us. His reply shewed him to be a gentleman, and one who was passionate about his chosen medium. The fact that he returned the poem I enclosed shews that he was kind and intelligent. Presumably he could not bring himself to destroy an item of verse, however bad,

and there was no way he would want to keep it. I have reread it – it is truly execrable: but Masefield's words of encouragement have stayed with me all my life.

Manqué

Manqué is a word borrowed from the French because we have nothing like it. 'Would-be' is close but lacks the undertones and overtones of pathos.

If you are a passionate Poet then it drives you all the time. You do not write the Poems; the Poems write you. It does not follow that the Poetry is good, just that you will produce many reams of it. Manqué Poets just have Poetry in their soul and use it for special events as no other medium will do. Alas this also is no guarantee of quality.

These are a cross-section of Verses from throughout my life. A number of them have been sieved from the scree of my memory whereas a number have been lost over the years. There are also a number that have not been included because they are too personal – eulogies, poems of thanks, welcome and so forth. Those included are for a more general audience. The ones selected still amuse me. But then, in the words of Mandy Rice-Davies, they would, wouldn't they? I just hope that they amuse you too.

Maturation

There is no date order in these pieces, although some my be datable from their content.

For a Lifetime reflection of a true Poet, the sequence of output could be relevant, shewing the subtle maturing of talent. On the other hand the greatest works are often at the start of the career when youthful imagination and daring flourish. If you doubt this, consider a parallel art form – consider the Rolling Stones. They have been writing and performing for half a century, yet if you ask anyone to name their favourite track it will probably be from the 60s.

For the occasional Poet these rules do not apply. The Verse is of the Time and, in reverse, the Time is of the Verse. And the chance of maturity is approaching Nil.

Metre

The majority of these verses are in rhyme. The rhyme schemes are very basic. I use rhyme mainly because it imposes another layer of complexity upon composition which better focuses the mind.

It also makes verses easier to recall, and is in essence more satisfying. Sometimes unrhyming verse can be the very irritating. Consider the following impromptu offering which could have been a Limerick:

> *There was an old man who once fell*
> *Perversely into a deep hole.*
> *His friends, with great hopes*
> *To help, threw down lines*
> *Should he not be piecemeal but sound.*

Musings

The proem at the start of this book is written by me for me. My memory is not bad but, not being a professional quizzer, it tends to lose its way in lists. Try yours. Name the seven Disney dwarves. If you run true to normal patterns you should get the first five fairly fast, struggle over the sixth and stall over the seventh. Which is usually Bashful. Then try the actors of 'The Magnificant Seven'. The point is that without some form of mnemonic I would never remember the nine Muses and their specialities but now I always do: let me share them with you.

Throughout this book there are a few paragraphs opposite a number of the Verses which refer to the reasons for their composition. These are just me chatting to you. They are peepholes into someone else's life and may be completely disregarded. I primarily hope that you enjoy the Poems.

JJS May 2018

We start with a Birth. Not my own, although a hippie friend once told me, charmingly, that an embryo sang and danced throughout its time in the womb. I imagine that such Terpsichorean activities cease abruptly with a welcoming slap on the back.

The awe comes when the natural process, which is accelerating this planet to the seven-and-a-half billion mark, simplifies down to two. The newborn creation of someone close to you becomes a magical form of miniaturised perfection as yet untrammelled by Life.

I returned home and wrote 'Transylvanian Lullaby'.

It is pointless trying to express strong emotions, at best they will come out as maudlin. If you want to reach the whole world then write nonsense verse which is always for everyone. Even if they don't see it. Or even, if they have the good sense to buy this book, they do.

Edward Lear behaved similarly though in a vastly different direction. Read 'The Courtship of the Yonghy-Bonghy-Bo', an amusing piece of Nonsense. Now read one of his biographies and reveal the circumstance under which he wrote it. Then try reading the Poem again without a lump in your throat.

But, as I said, we were writing from different perspectives. Lear was exhaling Grief: I was inhaling Joy. To this end I dedicate this volume to both Mother and Child (q.v.), even if it is a little late in the day.

Transylvanian Lullaby

Hush little baby, now don't you cry
Though the wind is wild and the vampires fly:
Your Daddy's draping garlic round the windows for your sake
And he's sharpening a point on a hickory stake.

Smile little baby, now don't you scowl
Though the moon is full and the werewolves prowl:
Your Daddy is a marksman second to none
And he's moulding silver bullets for his hunting gun.

Peace little baby, you're safe at home
Though the thunder roars and the monsters roam:
Your Daddy's in the castle on the crag close by
And he's cutting off their electricity supply.

Sleep little baby, everything's fine
Nothing's going to harm a baby of mine.
You're going to live long and you're going to be rich
'Cos your Daddy is a mummy – and your Mummy is a witch!

'Songs of Embarrassment' was my first anthology and a handful of my favourites are scattered throughout this book. They are based on the fact that for some the fear of Social Embarrassment is greater than the fear of just about anything including Death.

It was initially inspired by a local newspaper report of an elderly lady who, while out shopping, tripped over in the street. Several people helped her up, but she waved, saying she was fine, and walked home briskly. When she reached home she was still in pain and it transpired that she had broken her leg.

The verse opposite 'wrote itself' in the car whilst I was making a short trip to meet a friend and I enjoyed it so much that many others followed.

In reading through, I find an unsurprising masculine slant, but the Embarrassment are all taken from the feminine point of view. The emotions of social unease transcend gender, but the female expression of it is more prevalent and deeper.

Bones

Songs of Embarrassment 1

My doggie keeps on digging up old bones in the backyard
And he *will* bring them in the house although I scold him hard.
It's true he's been good company since Hubby's been away
But, missing master's voice, he grows more difficult each day.
Oh no, he's brought another in! Now, if I've not lost track,
He only has to find the skull and I'll have Hubby back.

I composed this in the half mile walk from a station to a friend's house. During an uneventful train journey I had been contemplating the parable repeated by the Venemous Bede about Life resembling a sparrow flying from a stormy night into a mead hall, through the bright hall and then back into the outer darkness.

I had never thought this a very good analogy as it precludes personal options, and I was then considering it better to think in terms of a Life Train. You board it at the Request Stop of your birth, you cannot leave it and you disembus at the Terminus with your name on it. The train carries on without you.

Now this realization of a future without yourself, in your own eyes, as a central character is unusually downbeat, so I set myself the task of composition to restore my mood.

The Moral is that you should enjoy all present experiences and cherish their memory, but that you should Never, Never Go Back.

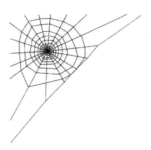

Never Go Back

A Half-a-Mile Verse

I searched the attic and I found
Amidst the mildew and the must
A mobile made of memories,
Of cobwebs, shadow-shards and rust.
But even as I watched, it swirled
With sudden swiftness into dust.

I searched the cellar and I found
Beneath the fallen flakes of lime
A figure fashioned out of fears
And fancies, fungus-flesh and grime.
But even as I watched, it sank
With sullen slowness into slime.

I searched the chambers in between,
I roamed through each and every room
To find a tapestry of life and laughter
Ripped from Love's lost loom.
But all the walls were cracked and bare
Like those upon a time-worn tomb.

This was my first public demonstration of Spontaneous Verse. You ask for a Title, a Theme or a First Line and then compose a verse whilst you are reciting it.

We have all in our heads a mishmash of topics and rhymes which can be plagiarised – the trick is to have a rough idea of where the verse is going, keep at least two lines ahead of your recitation and declaim v e r y s l o w l y.

This is scary. You are putting yourself in the position of a dreamscape which I have inhabited a couple of times, quite common to actors, of being thrust onto a Stage and not knowing your lines. This is not because stagefright has caused you to forget them but because you never learned them and *have no idea what the Play is*.

I did not try Spontaneous Verse very often and I believe that this, my first attempt, was probably my best.

Instant Nightmare

Spontaneous Verse

Last night
I dreamed a dream in jagged black
Past fright
I fled before a ragged pack
Of
Shifting shadows, flitting forms
Shapeless serpents, writheless worms
Zo-ons oozing from the slime
From outer space and out of time
Out of sync and out of sump
From every mental rubbish dump
Out of sight, out of my mind
Thoughts I thought I'd left behind
Behind me now and closing fast
Fears for Future, frights from Past
But now their Presence scared me
Now
As my mind began to slow
And
Fate-fettered feet began to flag
And
Shock-shaken shell began to sag
And
I came upon a cosmic chasm
My body arced, sparked by a spasm
I...
Woke up!
How will I ride my nightmare road?
Soak up
Tonight's exciting episode!

Pieces

Songs of Embarrassment 2

I love to decorate our flat (I'm into Objet Troove)
With sticks and stones and bricks and bones – Piers never did approve.
I found this lovely rusty Shape and brought it home with care.
It made a super centrepiece – but Piers went simply spare!
He positively kicked the thing (he was a little tight).
I didn't know it was a bomb – but serves him jolly right.

The next four poems are from my last anthology entitled 'Animal's Kin'. This is as close as it gets to pure Nonsense Verse: my favourite verseform that is incredibly easy to write badly and ineffably hard to write well. One tries to follow in the foolscap of 'Jumblies' Lear, 'Snark' Carroll and 'Capital Ship' Carryl but one fails – they should be held aloft as a target to aim for.

Oh all right! When I write this is my 'last' anthology I should point out that the number of works between my first and last is precisely zero. But 'the last' rather than 'the other' makes it seem that there are several more in my lifetime that I have casually discarded, and so cuts down upon the true obviousness of my poetic manqiness.

Bear-Faced Robbery

Should you cross the Unjust Desert 'til you reach the Eighth Oasis
Do not linger there for longer than a lungful of fresh air;
For there bides a band of bearfolk that are bald, bad, bold and bawdy –
They will rob you of your clothing, for they haven't any hair!

They wear antiquated anklets round their Arthuritic ankles,
They wear armbands ripped from uniforms of land and sea and air,
They wear boaters and blue blazers boasting big bright brassy buttons,
They wear chainmail and cheap chapeaux, but they haven't any hair!

They wear dapper DJ's djs, they wear dinner suits with dickeys,
They wear evening gowns with furbelow, with flounces and with flair,
They wear once-flip floppy flip-flops, they wear alligator gaiters,
They wear sacking hacking jackets, but they haven't any hair!

They wear real cool creamy ice-shoes, they wear yoicks-and-tally jodhpurs,
They wear kaftans with great caution, they wear kilts with utmost care,
They wear leotards from leopards and loincloths purloined from lions,
They wear mini-monokinis, but they haven't any hair!

They wear monocles and nonocles (which baffle most opticians)
They wear opaque pincenez-quizzing glasses which are *very* rare,
They wear rough and ragged raglans, they wear sorry-looking saris,
They wear too, too tattered tutus, but they haven't any hair!

They wear umpteen underclothing, they wear vests of vivid velvet,
They wear waistcoats lined with whalebone which reduces wear and tear,
They wear X-fronts, Y-fronts, Z-fronts (the last word in nether garments),
They wear yashmaks, they wear zoot suits, but they haven't any hair!

So beware the Unjust Desert and avoid the Eighth Oasis;
Should you fall among the bearfolk you will be the one that's bare!
They will rob you of your raiment, they'll divest you from your vestments;
You'll continue on your journey wearing nothing... but your hair!

This was originally entitled 'Ewe-topia' but it did not seem quite to fit.

I apologise for the elongation of the final she-ee-ee-eep.

The difference between some poetry and song is minimal. When a poem has a simple beat it often approaches a chant in recital, and I can no longer reach the end of this one without feeling the roll of organ chords at the end of 'Dead Puppies' by Ogden Edsl.

It was the Baamy Sheep which principally prompted my Partner and my Publisher to persuade me to prepare this pamphlet. I am not sure why, as I do not think this Verse is one of my strongest, but my ego is very grateful and this book is Dedicated to them both (q.v.)

Sheer Sheep

Oh! The Baamy Sheep, the Baamy Sheep
Keep clear of the Baamy Sheep!
Each one is stronger than a bull
Their coats are made of wire wool
They're gruff and rough and tough as nails
They chase the dogs and bite their tails
So canny canines turn and creep away from the Baamy Sheep.

Ooh! The Baamy Sheep, the Baamy Sheep
You will never find asleep!
They are always wide awake
They are always on the make
The Lambs that gambol in the Spring
Will fleece you out of everything
The cost of living is not cheap amongst the Baamy Sheep.

Oooh! The Baamy Sheep, the Baamy Sheep
They're the ones that mugged BoPeep!
They drink old Sheep Dip 'til they're tight
Then go out spoiling for a fight
At free-form fighting they're the tops
Fell foes with wicked mutton chops
And leave them lying in a heap, those lamb-bam-Baamy Sheep.

Ooooh! The Baamy Sheep, the Baamy Sheep
Enough to make a willow weep!
You never find these Sheep in flocks
Unless they're out a-hunting Fox
Or else with wolfskins on their backs
They try to infiltrate Wolf packs
Prudent predators all leap away from the Baamy Sheep.

Oooooh! The Baamy Sheep, the Baamy Rams
The Baamy Ewes, the Baamy Lambs!
Into their secrets do not pry
Their favourite dish is Shepherd Spy
No weapons work against this horde
The sheep pen's mightier than the sword
So keep your head and always keep away from the Baamy She-ee-ee-eep.

HISTORICAL NOTE: The line 'Not one speaks in praise of Bacon' refers to the delightful 'Ode to Tobacco' (read it!) by Calverley.

Bacon Brothers Tobacconists was founded in the same year as the Battle of Trafalgar and had a high-quality shop in Cambridge until sadly it closed in 1983.

The line 'Here's to thee, Bacon!' is the last in Calverley's 1862 poem. Bacon Brothers were so taken with the verse that they named one of their Special Mixtures after him; and a bronze plaque bearing his portrait and his poem is attached to the wall of the shop.

It is still there today though the shop is now one specializing in ladies lingerie.

From Briars to Bras.

Such is the Bias of Brass, as a Yorkshireman might say.

The Country of the Swine

In the Bay of Pigs they sip syrup of figs
(Not one knows the slang for beer)
And they brill in the brine, for it chills the spine,
'Neath the pines whence the Shylarks peer.
All their wigs they tip as they make the trip
To their rigorous midday meals
Where they swink and swill with a wink and a will
And delirious squabbish squeals.

In the Land of Boars they munch petits fours
(Not one ever mentions pork)
And they mull in the mud, for it warms the blood,
Near the suds where the Woefowl squawk.
All their straws they doff as they near the trough
For their raucous evening revels
Where they all cavort with a grunt and a snort
On several different levels.

On the Isle of Hogs they smoke purple fogs,
(Not one speaks in praise of Bacon)
And they rail in the rain, for it clears the brain,
On the plains where the Grice are forsaken.
All their clogs they shed as they go to bed
In their soggy, straw-strewn pits
Where they sleep 'til dawn with a snore and a yawn
And occasional coughing fits.

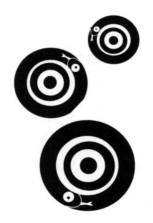

Serpendipity

On the Island of Haymaka where the sun forever shines
Where the Jeepers Creepers flourish and the gaudy Yourdi Vines
There are countless curious creatures but the strangest of them all
Is the family of Serpents that have never learnt to crawl.

Each morning when they waken they curl themselves in loops
And, tail-tips gripped in teeth-tips, they bowl around like hoops.
They roll down to the ocean, they have no need of sails
But skim along the shallows, propelled by twirling tails.

At noontide when they're peckish they surf out of the sea
And wrap themselves like decorations on a Hissmass Tree.
They dine on bark and berries, on sawdust and on sap,
On Houndstooth Caterpillers – whatever they can trap.

To help digest their luncheon they coil themselves around
In counter-clockwise spirals until they're fully wound
Then, flexing all their muscles, they *spring* into the air
And bounce around the island without a single care.

They bounce until its twilight and the sun is not so hot
When they congregate together and form one giant knot
And thus they sleep contented, each happy little snake
Aware that in the morning it's still Spring-time when they wake!

On the Island of Haymaka where wild Punches do no harm
Where the Omnibushes blossom and the seedy Reedya Palm
There are hordes of happy creatures, but the happiest of all
Is the family of Serpents that have never learnt to crawl.

Shocks

Songs of Embarrassment 3

My twins both watch this programme and now they *must* be vets,
And if thay wasn't bad enough they want such dreadful pets!
Last month it was a wallaby, last week a baby seal,
And this week they just had to have a live electric eel.
They left it in poor Nana's bath – it shocked her to the core –
Now 'til I've paid the funeral bills they won't get any more.

The Minack Theatre is an open air venue in Cornwall on a Porthcurno clifftop just up the road from Lands End.

This magical place is the brainchild of the late, great Rowena Cade who designed and built the theatre aided only by her gardener. If you do not know this stunning undertaking, commenced in the 1930s, look at its internet site which, apart from History and News, includes a fulltime webcam of the Stage.

Since the 1950s, it has been producing a gradually lengthening Season of weeklong plays by groups from all over the country and occasionly from abroad. I was involved for 15 years with two of the companies, and was asked for 1978 if I could write an adaptation of 'Canterbury Tales' for production by the Hertfordshire Players.

With the confidence and arrogance of youth I said 'No problem' and produced five of the Tales linked in rhyming decameter couplets. It was actually a fun form to work with , and the other great joy was writing one's own character in one of the scenes.

The extract here appended is the Prologue of the Reeve's Tale, told as part of a bickering feud between the Miller and he. (A Reeve was a high-up official of a district – the word Sheriff derives from Shire-Reeve). It has the advantage of being a longish piece by one actor rather than distractingly by many.

This was the first year that the Minack produced its annual trophy for the best play of the season and, *mirabile dictu*, Hertfordshire Players won it!

It has since been performed by a number of groups, won the Felixstowe Festival and has been aired at the Edinburgh Festival. Its last outing was the hugely successful 2017 Summer Tour by the Taunton Thespians.

It is reassuring to know that good old Mediaeval Sex & Violence does not date!

Pilgrimmorality

Extract from The Reeve's Prolog

At Trumpington, near Cambridge, stood a mill
And you may see it for it stands there still
Straight through the village down beside the water.
There lived a Miller with his wife and daughter;
There was a baby in a cot as well
And it is of these four I'm going to tell.
The Miller in this story, you will find,
Is very lifelike, very true to kind –
In short a boasting bully and a bragger
And known by one and all as 'Sim the Swagger'
For he would flaunt himself about the place.
Yet no-one dared deride him to his face
For though his wits weren't sharp he compensated –
With dagger, sword and knife his belt was weighted
And anyone who made a foolish joke
Could find his punchline cut off at a stroke.
His wife was cast in much the selfsame mould.
She always sniffed as though she had a cold
To shew her disapproval and her scorn
Of those that she considered 'lowly-born'
(Though none were lower born than she in life)
But now she primped it as the Miller's wife
And none dared call her anything but 'Madam' –
If they had tried it Simkin would have had 'em.
Yet it was often whispered, with some truth,
That she has been quite pretty in her youth
And she would doubtless be all right in bed –
At night and with a flour sack on her head!
The daughter on the other hand was finer
And though too coarse to be compared to china
She could be called a pretty piece of pottery.
She had received in Nature's private lottery,
Which allocates some losses and some gains,
Twice mother's looks but half her father's brains –

Twice mother's looks
but half her father's brains

In short she was a stupid girl but beautiful;
She was, moreover, daughterfully dutiful
And always did whatever parents said
And as her mother meant her to be wed
To some rich lord she'd never had a taste
Of making love, which was a shocking waste.
Virginity's like newly minted gold
If left until it's tarnished and grown old
It is devalued – it's a false economy
It should be spent when young with joy and bonhomie,
For though your principles may disappear
The interest will remain for many a year!
About the baby I will be quite short
But merely state it was an afterthought;
In fact it quite surprised the Miller's wife
Because old Sim was getting on in life
And though he strutted like a farmhouse rooster
He didn't act the part as once he used'ta!
You'll find in fact this saying very true:
'The more men flaunt themselves the less they do'
And Simkin was the vainest of God's creatures.
Yet every man, you say, has some good features.
About his many faults you've heard me tell
But... was he honest? Was he bloody Hell!

The second Play I penned for the Minack was commissioned neither by the Theatre nor by the Players. It was a concept I had neen nursing for decades which finally coalesced in my mind. It was 'Murder at the Minack' and takes place over three consecutive seasonal plays.

The first Act opens with the first Act of 'The Importance of being a Woman' – the third in Oscar Wilde's Importance trilogy. The embedded Play ends abruptly with an onstage murder.

The first Act ends with the second Act of Shakespeare's Historical Tragedy 'Xerxes' from which the lines opposite are extracted. It too ends in tragedy.

The Hertfordshire Players accepted it and submitted it to the Minack who turned it down (Rowena Cade is now deceased, but had thoughtfully set it up as a Charitable Trust) on the grounds that the playwright was not well known. It was replaced by a production by that writer so well known to English audiences - Bertold Brecht.

If you detect a hint of bitterness, it is actually sadness. If they had said that the writing was rubbish that would have been disappointing but acceptable ('Huh! What do they know of True Talent?')

However, to write a piece which can only be played at one location in the entire world and having it refused by that place on political grounds emphasizes once again the aptness of the word 'manqué'.

Xerxes
– the Power Speech

An Extract of an Extract

Life's but a Game, and Power moves the pieces,
The Power that is tatooed on our Souls.
The Power of a father o'er his son,
The Power of the son o'er his young babe,
The Power of the babe o'er his grandsire
(The subtlest one of all) and all reciprocal.
From these first nurs'ry blocks the Power starts;
Each man is judged upon his family
For Power is perceived to flow with blood.
So use thy family, but mark thy sons.
The next great Power is the font of Lust,
It deeper runs than kinship or than love.
A single word can quite o'erthrow a man
Who governs thousands, ruined in a trice
By She whom the besotted fool encraves.
Lust is the animal within us all
So fight it not – but give it not free rein.
Carpe Feminam! for men of power
Take off whatever pieces might object
As husband, father – so the game is played.
Now, having overskied these basic hurdles,
Review thyself and analyze thy strengths
Of breeding, wit, command and martial art
Of popularity and cunning tongue..
Employ them each and every day, because
The more that Power's used the more it grows.
The Man of Power grasps whate'er he needs.
The idler says 'But take away these vantages
And I am good as he' To him I trow
'Thy might is could-have-been: my Might is now!'
Now, having scaled the pinnacle of Power
Surround thyself with Potent ministers
For weak men undermine a kingdom's health.

Life's but a Game,
and Power moves the pieces

But play each piece the one against the other
And use their weaknesses to prove thy might.
Anent a general wield harsh Diplomacy,
Around a vizir build a wall of Force,
And to a chief-priest pose Reality.
Thus in this way their Power magnifies
The Power that is thine. The Game is won.
Now use this Superpower 'gainst the gods:
From out their pool of Worship take great draughts
And so reflect their Glory to thyself.
The games that gods play are exceeding slow
And though their Vengeance may fall in the end
Until it does men think thou hast their blessing,
So let their Silence be a blessing on thee...

Scene

Songs of Embarrassment 4

Yes, I did kill my husband – but I was *very* harassed –
He always had this dreadful knack of making me embarrassed.
He found me with the coalman (we were resting on the bed)
And he began to make a scene – I won't say what he said.
Now that would have been bad enough if it had been a friend –
But not in front of tradesmen, that really was the end!

I was in a pub which had imported some live folksingers for the night. They were very tuneful and had quite a large appreciative audience.

There was one male singer who rendered a couple of numbers *a cappella*. He sang, unfocussed on the audience, bent over the mike with a hand cupped around an ear, which I am told gives one perfect feedback. Moreover, to a near tone-deaf Philistine such as I, the songs sounded the same even though one was about the bloody murder of his family by English soldiers and the other was about his lovelorn feelings for the Laird's daughter.

I am afraid that I found this very funny, and I wrote the ballad opposite later. The rough date of this can be gathered from the phrase 'Marital Aids' which was then the coy name for sex toys and had acquired none of its pejorative overtones.

Whether it was as amusing as it was intended to be is a moot point, but it reduced one lady friend of the time into fits of laughter and out of her clothes.

The Pedlar Of Pleasure

A Folk Ballad

I met an old pedlar, his wares on his back,
Dark glasses he wore and a dirty white mac.
I asked him his business, he peered through his shades
And said I'm a pedlar of Marital Aids.

Come all you brave Squires and all you bold Jades,
Oh come all you Old Folk before all hope fades,
Oh come all you Bachelors, come all you Maids,
Oh come all and sample my Marital Aids.

He said what I've got is the stuff of your dreams
Virility potions, fertility creams,
I've items to please you when you're on your own
There are some made of leather and some of whalebone.

Come all you brave Squires and all you bold Jades,
Oh come all you Old Folk before all hope fades,
Oh come all you Bachelors, come all you Maids,
Oh come all and sample my Marital Aids.

Now if you are old and have had a hard life
And have taken in marriage a lovely young wife
I have here an object on which you may strap
Which will pleasure your spouse while you're taking a nap.

Come all you brave Squires and all you bold Jades,
Oh come all you Old Folk before all hope fades,
Oh come all you Bachelors, come all you Maids,
Oh come all and sample my Marital Aids.

If business necessities cause you to roam
And you find yourself sleeping a long way from home
I have here a box that's a substitute mate
Provided its contents you've breath to inflate.

Oh come all and
sample my Marital Aids.

Come all you brave Squires and all you bold Jades,
Oh come all you Old Folk before all hope fades,
Oh come all you Bachelors, come all you Maids,
Oh come all and sample my Marital Aids.

So I bid him adieu and he went on his way
Peddling pleasure to all who were willing to pay.
He sold me a salve to improve my prowess –
Any sceptical maiden may have my address!

So all you brave Squires and all you bold Jades,
We're the King of the Bachelors, Queen of the Maids.
Let us treasure each other 'til energy fades
True love and true lust need no Marital Aids.

A friend of mine was compiling an anthology on the Hare. I lent her some book illustrations of an animal I have long admired. I also, unsolicited, composed the verse opposite which I sent to her.

Was it good enough to fit into the anthology? We will never know, as it arrived past the submission date.

She said it was splendid and would have been included had it arrived in time, but she is a lovely person and would have said that anyway. I choose to believe it, and am sorry to miss the anthology.

Writing it was hare-raising, though.

Hare Today

The Hare, he is Immortal: myth-murmured, ballad-sung
His ears, his brain, his upper lip, all parts of the English tongue.
His legs are Nature's legacy and legendary for luck
His fleetness is his fortune for none can pass the buck.
There is nobody and nothing that the Hare cannot outrun
This the Hare knows; but tomorrow comes the hunter with his gun.

The Hare, he's independant: never tied to wife or child
A carefree creature of the world, a freeman of the wild.
A natural Lothario, his life's a playboy's dream
Collecting setts of docile does within his Hare harem.
Without commitment life's a round of neverending fun
This the Hare knows; but tomorrow comes the hunter with his gun.

The Hare, he is inquisitive: and none can say him no
He has a nose for mystery, he simply has to *know*.
He has to know what's around each hedge and what's behind each door
His life's a tale of hare-breath 'scapes on land and field and moor.
He's unearthed a hundred secrets and he's only just begun
This the Hare knows; but tomorrow comes the hunter with his gun.

The Hare's a handsome hero: though his enemies abound
There is not a one among them that can run the Hare to ground.
He leaves the fox dog-tired, he leaves the hounds outfoxed
He's well aware of each hare-snare; he'll box but not be boxed
He knows the keeper's vermin rack and doesn't give a hang
'Til tomorrow comes...
                tomorrow comes...
                    tomorrow comes...
                        and ****

Gun Tomorrow

These are Haiku, a traditional Japanese verseform consisting of three lines containing 5 7 5 syllables. They are meant to encapsulate a special vision of Nature or a blinding metaphysical insight.

What my two examples encapsulate is that I do not fully understand their point.

This is like watching a French play. One may appreciate the setting, the acting, and understand what they are doing – but is left wondering why they are doing it. Even something as well known as 'Cyrano de Bergerac', which leaves French audiences openly weeping in their seats, leaves their English counterparts finding his motivations baffling. The answer is 'because he is French'. This does not imply that the French are inferior or superior, just that they have different historical reactions.

Perhaps I should write
a poignant Haiku on this
or then perhaps not.

Dammit, I just have.
Haikus are insidious.
Blast – done it again!

Hairy Hippo Haiku

Samson at the Barbers

There Mister Samson
Shaved hairlessness becomes you
Tonsures lend one strength

Lovesome Leviathans

Hippopotami
Make love subaqueously
With vast tenderness

Clocks

Songs of Embarrassment 5

I found Jim's body on the floor, it came as quite a shock.
He'd slipped and fallen off the stool whilst trying to wind the clock.
I rang the Doctor and Police, changed into something black,
Then to my horror found Jim sitting up when I got back.
What could I tell the Doctor? I did feel such a fool!
And I couldn't face the policemen – so I brained Jim with the stool.

Some years ago two of the favourite people in my quirkiverse compiled a cycle of poems called '24 Hours'. I was privileged to have had included an introductory homage to Midnight – the mystic split between days (and moreover, the time of day when I fully come to life).

I dedicate this book to them both (q.v.)

It is the closest thing to Modern Verse that I have ever written, and is hugely improved by its concretised typesetting.

Zero Hour

ZERO HOUR

Is Nothing sacred?

Plas Tick

MidNight
High AntiNoon: the owls' prowl:
The stable sable morning:
The Hour of the Which

Please name
The style by which you're reckoned
Is it Nought or Twentyfour
Or is it inbetweenier?

Dim light
The shadow wolfcubs howl
The puppy is a-borning
Of Yesterday's dead bitch

High time
You realised that I am both
From OmyGod to Omega
2 Presents at a stroke

Freeze Frame!
For just one picosecond –
Caught between the Days' shared Jaw –
Chronoschizophrenia!

Why Rhyme?
I am the Hour without the Minutes
I am the No Hour the Minutes pass
I am All or Nothing

Plas Tock

And now I'm next to Nothing

NO TIME

Concrete Poetry is 'an arrangement of linguistic elements in which the typographical effect is more important in conveying meaning than verbal significance.'

That's a quote, and shouldn't be.

Concrete Poetry is basically Shaped Verse, and this has been around for 2000 years. The best known nowadays is the Mouse's Tale from 'Alice in Wonderland.'

This perVerse is an extension of the one I prepared for the Website of Zzota, my Game and Puzzle Company.

Time Square

Concrete Poetry
LIFE IS A GAME

LIFE'S	SAY	A	OTHERS	GAMING	WHAT	DISASTER	SCORN
WAY	THAT	YOUR	NO.ONE	IT	CAN	REACH	MASTER
PLAY	GOAL	IT	HIDDEN	WITH	ONE	LOVE	HAS
WHOLE	AND	A	ENJOY	AS	EVERY	LIFE	MOVE
RULES	QUEST	OF	THE	A	RELISH	GAME	AND
TEST	FOR	EVERY	EACH	ENJOY	THE	OS	SAME
EMPLOY	CRACK	YOUR	CAN	OWN	NO.ONE	RULES	THAT
ALACK	FOR	PUZZLE	LIVING	A	NOT	LIFE'S	FOOLS'

LIFE IS A PUZZLE
Discreet Pros

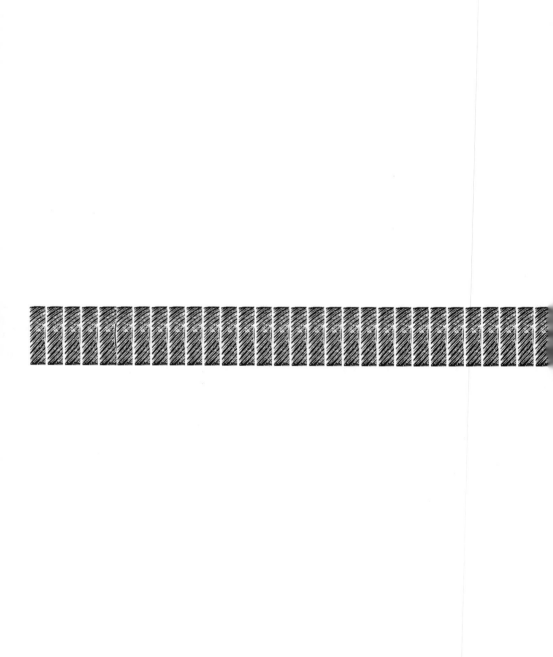

FREE
GIFTS!

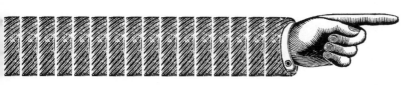

Some years ago, Cedric Lytton, a leading light in the British Chess Problem Society, published a book entitled 'Deceptive Chess Problems'. He included this apposite puzzle I wrote for him in the Introduction. Achesstic is a portmanteau word merging Acrostic and Chess.

Chess was a great influence in my early life. I played for both my College and my University, but my real interest was in Fairy Chess. Fairy Chess states that the board, pieces and rules of Chess are just one of an infinity of possibilities – so in Fairy Chess you get Hexagonal boards, Neutral Grasshopper pieces and Serieshelpstalemates.

If you want to try an interesting game, I suggest Alice Chess. This is played as normal chess but with two boards, the second one starting the game empty. When a legal move is made on one board the piece is moved to the identical square on the other board where it must also be legal. Learn to play this and you will defeat even County players who are baffled by it.

I was going to give a brief breakdown of the terms used in the Puzzle, but if you are in the zone you will know them as well as your mother's maiden name, and if you are not you would only be more confused. If you want to learn more buy ASM Dickens' splendid book 'A Guide to Fairy Chess'.

You do not need to understand the words to solve the Puzzle, you just need an open mind.

A Majestic Achesstic

FREE GIFT! – *Rattle Your Brain*

My 1st is in CHANGE
but not in MUTATE

My 2nd's in GRIMSHAW
and also CHECKMATE

My 3rd is in MODEL
and also IDEAL

My 4th is in SCHIFFMANN
but not in KNIGHTWHEEL

My 5th is in STALEMATE
but not in SUCCESS

My Whole is a board game –
but not what you'd guess!

My Answer is HALMA – not all games are CHESS!

I picked up a magazine in a Waiting Room and the back page was a lonely hearts log of men wanting the partnership of women. Their self-descriptions had the metallic tang of exaggeration and a number had entered in black and white that they owned a Rolex watch. A good few of them possessed a GSOH as well, but as this was self-evaluated it would be interesting to see how it translated into reality.

The ladies they were seeking should be attractive, intelligent, sensitive, sharing, good cooks and enjoy fun times and quiet evenings in with their prospective Rolex-owning partner. They presumably would also need a very GSOH to consider that somone with all their talents would be prepared to squander them on such a proposer. It would seem better for these male optimists to say that they owned a gold bar and had a lot of GOLD [Good Old La-Dida].

In the belief that Romance is more popular than Readies, to these unrequited dreamers I offer the verse opposite.

It also gives an outing to the Limerick which is a verseform I have always admired when well-handled. To this end I append for free two of my favourites, which properly belong to a subcategory called 'Gimmericks'

There was a Mod Poet of Kew
Whose Limericks stopped at line two.

but...

There was a mad Poet of Verdun.

Do-It-Yourself Seduction Kit

FREE GIFT! – Happiness is a Crutch Inc.

Not a lady alive is averse
To hearing their name in a verse:
Fill the gaps in each line,
And your love-life will shine –
(Or at least it won't get any worse).

My dearest Miss *[Please Insert Name]*
Who puts other ladies to shame
With your beautiful eyes
[Enter Number and Size]
And your fine *[Insert Portions of Frame]*

Since I saw you at quarter to three
In the year *[Enter Year Here]* A.D.
I can't sleep, I just dream –
Your complexion of cream
And *[Fruit Name]* fresh-picked from the tree.

So dearest Miss *[Name Here Once More]*
Your sweet smile makes archangels soar
And you're twitching my heart
With your fine *[Body Part]*
So reveal them to me I implore.

Envoi

Alas I must bid you farewell,
They've rung the bar-now-is-closed bell.
So, to any dear friend
Who has read to the end −
(Though unwise) without moans,
Without sighs, without groans
Who has not tossed this thin
Volume into the bin
Or the sad downstairs loo
And I reckon on TWO
(Total sum
Maximum) −
My thanks and this opus by me
I dedicate to you (q.v.)

Made in the USA
Lexington, KY
06 May 2018